COLORFUL WAS THEIR
VOICE

'. . . that great poem, which all

poets, like the co-operating

thoughts of one great mind,

have built up since the

beginning of the world'

P. B. Shelley, *A Defence of Poetry*

COLORFUL WAS THEIR VOICE

TWENTY-FIVE
AMERICAN
POETS

SHAHAR BRAM • NETA GOREN

sussex
ACADEMIC
PRESS
Brighton • Portland • Toronto

The right of Shahar Bram and Neta Goren to be identified as Authors of this work, and Neta Goren to be identified as Artist of the illustrations in this work, has been asserted in accordance with the Copyright, Designs and Patents Act 1988.

2 4 6 8 10 9 7 5 3 1

First published in 2013 in Great Britain by
SUSSEX ACADEMIC PRESS
PO Box 139
Eastbourne BN24 9BP

and in the United States of America by
SUSSEX ACADEMIC PRESS
920 NE 58th Ave, Suite 300
Portland, Oregon 97213-3786

and in Canada by
SUSSEX ACADEMIC PRESS (CANADA)
8000 Bathurst Street, Unit 1, PO Box 30010, Vaughan, Ontario L4J 0C6

British Library Cataloguing in Publication Data
A CIP catalogue record for this book is available from the British Library.

Library of Congress Cataloging-in-Publication Data
Bram, Shahar. Colorful was their voice : twenty-five American poets /
    Shahar Bram and Neta Goren.
pages cm
ISBN 978-1-84519-586-1 (h/b : acid-free paper)
1. Poets, American—Poetry. I. Goren, Neta. II. Title.
    PJ5055.17.R335C65 2013
    892.4'17—dc23

                                                          2012047523

Typeset & designed by Phil Barker.
Printed by TJ International, Padstow, Cornwall.

Contents

A Note to the Reader from the Poet and the Artist

This project began with a conversation. We were talking about Robert Lowell and John Berryman – the pain they suffered, the poetry they wrote. These two poets became a part of our life ever since Shahar wrote about them many years ago. The conversation went on, sporadically, during which we were surprised to find out each of us was keeping the dialogue going even when apart: Neta sketched a few lines in pencil, Shahar drafted a few words. We were both trying to portray a concise image that would render something of the poet and of the conversation.

Days turned into weeks and then months: the conversation kept going, more and more poets came to "visit", old dear friends we were glad to see and hear once again. Soon the sabbatical was over but the conversation continued and so we moved on with our project titled "Poets in Pencils": Discussing poetry and life, and then drafting on paper and panels of wood the faces of loved poets whose poems were part of our life since long. Soon enough they surrounded us, looking at us from Neta's drawings, and our small apartment became a community.

From these two or so years of conversation we picked twenty-five portraits. While the poets represented in *Colorful Was Their Voice* were carefully chosen, the selection in no way aims to embrace or represent any canon. Many great poets are not represented here if only for our failure to give them good enough colors and voice.

COLORFUL WAS THEIR VOICE

TWENTY-FIVE AMERICAN POETS

DELMORE SCHWARTZ

A generation's illness
is not an answer to a poet's death.
Each poet's sword - his soaring words,
yours were the ones that sang of solitude and silence,
a white birds' choir, the shooting stars
that crossed our heavens briefly
to realize their essence
in a dying consciousness.

If poetry is the expression of a burning
body, the humming orbit around
an obscure and twinkling core,
how long the pale wake lingers
on the mantle of night
after the heart fails?

In some hotel, lost fame, lost
man, and dead three days
of ignorance, the world
in which you flickered
gone, oh long ago,
an empty bottle in an empty room,
last drops of time consumed, of time
the monster and the pet you tamed and poked,
whose daughter love (the animal) your lines kept
circling, leaving room for others to step in.
Where are they now?

An empty circle,
an isolated talk against the wounded walls
of mind, the lullaby of holes, the horrors
splashed when all of a sudden
from a naked mirror a poet
young and promising reflects,
and poems old and strange
bubble up the brackish well of memory.
Did you believe in poetry
until the end, as was said?
Was poetry an ally
in the battle against a mental foe?
Could myth be an ally against oblivion?

ROBERT FROST

Even the strongest among us grows tired.
It is the night,
the mystery of a sylvan, snowy light
that finally bends him. The bold body
arches. A girl like the wind
closes the gate behind her and sails
through the garden. She touches the bark
with her fingers to hear the twisted tales
she doesn't quite understand but follows anyway:
they seem simple at first but suddenly interlace
like the threads in her mother's beautiful dress
whose colors, she feels, suit her small figure though she's new
to herself, lost and found at the same time.
She looks at her friend, his shape
is different but the same,
like a rainbow he is bent,
and yet colorful,
and still standing,
the garden is still safe:
time to climb up,
her storyteller is reaching for her.

H.D.

White face,
white thoughts,
white Greek hands,
where are you heading?
Back, carried away,
the sea snatched you,
forward, the old waves
winged your words,
displaced, the years drew you deeper,
up in the air a thousand ships flew,
your sculptured chariots sailed
to new ancient worlds.
Daughter of heavens and earth,
whirl your pointed pen, write

ALLEN GINSBERG

A Jewish Buddhist on a tenement roof:
hey, what is he doing there?
Leaves of love fall, faithless eyes open:
he's giving the violin Zen lessons-
I'm happy (he points the bow up)
and sad (he points his finger down):
could someone call the rabbi?
Could someone get the cops?

There's no need,
the city, a cracked mother,
cages him, New York cradles him
in her arms but soon the boy takes the lead,
they dance a wild and very soft dance,
the roofs swing, the streets howl, joy
and naked pain join, flowers of grace
in their wake: the journey has started,
to the stars,
to the open,
at once a whole generation is awake.

JAMES WRIGHT

Tall ears of wheat are rising,
a field expands its wings.
I walk among exploding clods,
a wanderer,
like a thin and blasted stalk I sway
to the rhythm of wheat.
Higher still they rise,
rows of limbs waiting
to unload their grief.
I tread upon the pleading ground
and suddenly I cannot stop
my rising: my body can't resist
the solid comfort of the soil
after the harvest.

LANGSTON HUGHES

People are singing,
their bodies sway,
their body is the fruit of their voice,
their soft, fluffy fiber glorifies the wind
unprotected: stripes of flesh, scattered souls.

Blessed be the blind earth that gathers all seeds,
the clear words that assemble torn cotton bolls:
both feet on the ground
a people is singing
in one voice

ELIZABETH BISHOP

Dear Elizabeth,
The postcards you sent us, those careful and colorful letters,
reflections of, and upon, nature's visions, city life, human heart
the imagined places you visited, sojourned, drew
a detailed, opaque and visible record of interior landscapes, you
bright, inquiring and very precise images, accumulate, and soon
as in the story, the map will cover the world, it transcends
any origin, beauty is a realm to itself, in which we follow
your pathways, dear traveler, with open eyes, the world
you present us with is indeed sometimes unfathomable,
and the mute questions keep rolling without rest like waves
on the painted shore, silent but glimmering-
please write us more,
Yours

CHARLES OLSON

It is still here, at this clash
of words with time, the given
land that my heart learnt
by heart while
reading
Gloucester
words harbor on the shores of this island
hands throwing nets
poets and fishermen struggling to be
one with the universe,
the on-going process without end,
the persistence that makes a place,
The Earth-and the sea level, Heaven
now, here, *I am making a mappemundo. It is to include*
my being the product of the process of reading,
living is an unpolished poetic practice
to become engaged
Gloucester
welcomes my footsteps
on his shore-
lines, his lanes,
physically, I am home. Polish it.

ROBERT LOWELL

Needles, nails, whipping-
someone's mind must be out of his –
it must be my body.
And shrinking,
once a Tsar
now a flat balloon;
the memory of flying,
and the fright of recalling my selves.
Ah but writing, the little time
left after the highs and I's
sliding down, the who I am
putting down.
The hangman and his victim are one

EZRA POUND

What went wrong?
Strong
the mad world
war roared, blasted
hope, so concrete was
the image, it became
abstract, so instant, beyond
time, so intimate,
void. The dynamo stopped,
slow, heavy, long words
in hell. Then the controversy
and so forth and who cares.
Genius, as a curse

DENISE LEVERTOV

She who loved
the reader
who assumed there is
   a secret
in a sudden line
who heard
a spoken word
in a bough or a beam
        in the wind
who marked
shadow of leaves
on leaves
and had faith
in its fine changing form
who prayed to the Muse
not to forsaken her
and sketched Mount Helicon
  (not that far,
     seen from the kitchen window)
again and again and
whose pen flared
  with the flame
    of the next poem
             each poem   the last poem
             each day   the first day
made the life of craft a flight of vocation:
putting it down it is no more the same,
transfigured, transformed, the spiritual hunger
finds an answer?
A wing breaks out of the hump,
I'm reading further in wonder

ROBERT CREELEY

What is the world
but a room
with two people
full of love and love
lost and a last
open window, an eye
and the dripping light
but bits of hope,
and the raindrops,
echoes of thoughts
wrapping us, joined
even when distanced,
in words, shining again
and again in love

WALT WHITMAN

shadowing the marsh
         the newborn world
the sun
    the reeds, old stalks
           through which
  the sphere looms, rising
the childman steps outside the opposition
the circle of life embraces life's contradiction
  the colorful, the sweetest
    word whispered, rippled, haloed
      through spears of grace
the moon
       the water reflects
    the sky   in the watching eyes
      the world

EMILY DICKINSON

The butterfly
is about to explode
with desire:
hushed colors,
compressed breaths,
little deaths,
bullets of heavenly passion,
fire

ROBERT HAYDEN

Freedom	I breathed through reading
Freedom	burning under my eyelids
Freedom	thick as the clouds
	I saw in my sleep
	upon which I could walk
Freedom	the whipping couldn't take away
	nor the kids' ostracization
	its flames gorging upon my air
Freedom	I saw clearly
	close at hand
	with my nearsighted eyes
visible Freedom	through writing
	I look into your eyes

HART CRANE

Consult your own experience, says Paul Valery,
and you will unavoidably conclude:
we understand each other, and ourselves,
thanks to our speedy passage over words.

Across the deep, the chasm
of thought and self consciousness,
runs a bridge.
To reach safely the other side
you must hurry along,
never look down, and keep away
from the shoulders; never send a leg into the thin air
to try a loose, heavenly dance.

Between one covering to the next, says Chaim Nachman Bialik,
the abyss blinks.
Crossing the thawing river
on the rickety bridge of wavering icicles, one must not linger
but leap rapidly, or else...

The sequence of words, the syntax of worlds,
an apparent comprehensible structure,
and contact, the contract of cause
and effect, origin and purpose,
a meaning, a bridge. Poetry,
a dance in mid-air, breaks
the chain, isolates
elements, under-
mines sense,
minds
movement itself.

Some, says Bialik, safely go in
on this bank and out on the other,
some poets look at the bottom and
make it in one piece. Swift, unfractioned
idiom, Brooklyn Bridge lured Hart to plunge
into the sigh of stars drifting on waters.
I see the lights glimmering
but I know the heart
of the poet lays bare in the deep,
walking on airy arches, poets
look into black.

WILLIAM CARLOS WILLIAMS

Pressed flowers in a book,
   hues and colors I once carried
      for you from the small garden,
leaving a wake of soft, coffee soil
   all the way to the kitchen,
    on which we had no choice but to tread,
dancing our way to the living room,
   for a vase, and then to the kitchen again,
     to fill it with fresh, shining water,
the sound of which greening
      in my mind like the stems
         I held under the cold stream,
memories,
  will they retain
    the sweet smell of the love
          of life
           we shared?

JOHN BERRYMAN

And so, the two of them kept
teasing each other and didn't notice
me much, not much of an audience,
an imaginary child
in a life-size dream,
quite a show, Mr. H., Mr. B.,
and the child,
and somewhere there was an I,
the mask of the poet
on my behind,
what a laugh,
bursting like a gunshot,
rolling like a falling father,
my – far away – heavy daughter,
and the bridge fly
fly

ANNE SEXTON

Not myself, anyway.
A mannequin
or a skeleton;
perhaps a doll.
I dress it, undress it,
I feed it with thoughts
which I afterwards share,
they spread like snakes in the air.
My fellow puppets are sympathizing,
'you remind me of someone I once met,' says the wolf,
and Rumpelstiltskin grins: 'I'm for real, I pay with gold.'
And indeed this is not a dream,
and I keep stitching my self,
smiling like hell.
I am so much awake,
I'm lying in the clearing,
a beautiful model
covered with empty leaves.
Go ahead, read through me,
I'm transparent,
you'll never see
I am not

RANDALL JARRELL

It's a beautiful road, says the child.
The player piano plays,
the boy's fingers follow the keys'
inexplicable life.
Mama? Pop? Wonders the teen,
a mockingbird sings, a mockingbird
can sound like anything.
A young man tracks down his footsteps
in a quest whose end is its beginning.
Life cracks open, a broken face
blooms in the man's face. The child
is father of the poet.

To everything there is a season
and there is a season everything
falls back to: dear sincerity,
break through the masks!
A bearded smile,
in a world without walls:
whoever you are, I believe you.

Unlike the player piano,
once played, the lost world
is lost. A child walked here,
sings the mockingbird,
it's a beautiful road.
The traffic's heavy.
He's about to cross.

T. S. ELIOT

Father Time echoes in the desert,
lonely cycles vibrate in his voice,
his hands tell us our way is one
and the same.

Empty and rich with past treasures
we walk, lost soldiers.
The wind laughs, oh so scarce.
The skeletal dogs keep silent as we pass.
We march on, we march as one.

Lord of our worldly slow soles,
is that you?
The sand in the hourglass whimpers,
we listen, falling grains, a faint thunder
without lightning.
We march the vast times.
We treasure words.

THEODORE ROETHKE

Inorganic matter, syllables
dancing, the syntax of search,
the grammar of growing, metaphysical
budding, the language of plants
the child learnt: my form is my substance.

Open the gates!
See the white light soothing
the heads of the chrysanthemums;
my drawn heart,
a greenhouse turning dark,
a streaked glasshouse I struggle
to illuminate, my shadows pinned
against your sweating walls.

SYLVIA PLATH

"Dr. Tod Mr. Gott Sir Liebhaber
will perform three farewell shows
starting this Spring, when the blossoming
red cells desire more, encore,
in the local theater Das Leben.
There will be no rerun."

"As in a colorful dream
the audience will have a rare opportunity
to watch the one and only
Der Heilige Vater
substantiate his three personalities.
There will be no rerun."

"Herr Teufel and Dame Seele
will sing Valediction,
dance the great tango,
unite and make flesh
in a beautiful maiden body.
There will be no rerun."

"Der Zeit, the Master of ceremonies,
will lead the last show
to be held on a bloody cold day
in a dense cell
when the theater is closed.
There will be no rerun."

ROBERT DUNCAN

In a field I saw
the host of images
his head a universe
his mouth the visions
of the uncompromised Real

A dreamer I saw
dancing and sowing
the furrows and fairies
grew out of his fingers
and flew into my fascination

A tree and his head
in heaven his roots
in mud his trunk
a ladder upon which
the angelkids climb up and down

Colorful was his voice
saying I must not miss
but experience the One
in its multiflorous form
a process, a poetry that won't stop

I woke up with this blossoming bud

ROBERT PENN WARREN

How long does it take a poet to find his own voice?
How many words must he taste? How many false
wings melt in the flight? Until a new music breaks
him, a new language orders him out
of his body, he couldn't tell he was locked
in a foreign form,
he spoke the poets' talk.

Aging on thin air, already
crowned, the eye still looking
for prey, finding its own body
a form.

The long flight of the gull, and not a fruitless one, and then
the white wing scythed the bright stalks of altitude
down, they were cut at the root, suddenly against the falling
sky a hawk *shudders to hold position in the blazing wind*
and his eye sees
the rock is a rock
the dry leaf is dry
the harsh land means only itself, at last
he knows the world is
the words are
his own. In one eye he arrows
the place where nothing is

And I,
whose language do I speak?